LESSONS *from* LIFE

Phoolmatee Dubay

Lessons from Life
Copyright © 2020 by Phoolmatee Dubay

Library of Congress Control Number: 2020914729
ISBN-13: Paperback: 978-1-64749-211-3
          Epub   978-1-64749-212-0

All rights reserved. No part of this publication may be reproduced, distributed, or transmitted in any form or by any means, including photocopying, recording, or other electronic or mechanical methods, without the prior written permission of the publisher or author, except in the case of brief quotations embodied in critical reviews and certain other noncommercial uses permitted by copyright law.

Although every precaution has been taken to verify the accuracy of the information contained herein, the author and publisher assume no responsibility for any errors or omissions.No liability is assumed for damages that may result from the use of information contained within.

Printed in the United States of America

GoToPublish LLC
1-888-337-1724
www.gotopublish.com
info@gotopublish.com

Giving In

Misery loves company
But being in misery
Would lead me to seeing another's misery

At a glance,
His eyes showed hurt
It was then that I understood he needed help with his
Realizing I had to share in his pain

He needed spoken words of comfort
But I had to cue in too the emotions that I saw
Then deciding to help
By understanding that he needed comforting without
saying anything

The course of actions I would take would not be words
But a gesture to say
Look at me?
I am here!

While reassuring him that all would be right
Within an hour
What seemed like eternity?
Within that hour
It would change!

Uniqueness

*I learnt that every woman is unique
As each one is different
Because of her unique attributes and qualities*

*The uniqueness of a woman is knowing that she belongs
While her ways should say who she is
Her success on the other hand would say she is accomplished
While her looks add to her beauty*

*As women we are members of our family
How so?
Because we have parents and maybe even siblings
But when we coexist with another, we then create our own family
We belong too*

*As a woman my ways spells who I am
As a woman I am a caregiver
Which allows me to be supportive,
And have everyone's interest at heart I know and care for*

*Women are generally successful
Because of the roles we play so well
It may include being a mother, wife, or professional
But no matter what the role she plays she is a success*

*Whereas a woman's beauty says
She is a confident woman
A woman to be admired
As she is*

I Learnt to Be Human

Sensitivity I lacked until I needed to know
Respect I showed then I received
Love I did not know was in others
Support I found in friends
Kindness I showed but did not know
Compassion led to love
Understanding meant that I knew
Knowledge I learnt I received

Learning About Oneself

I did not know myself until I learnt from unhappiness
And while experiencing happiness with others
Those were moments that brought meaning to my life
As I learnt more about myself

Unhappiness were times that taught me about sorrow, hopelessness, and darkness in my life
Sorrow came with the loss of loved ones
Hopelessness made it seemed like I had no future of my own
Darkness came from drugging and drinking

Happiness were moments that taught me about love, laughter, and overcoming
Love came with the birth of my nieces
Laughter came from the humor of friends that made me smile
Overcoming meant that sorrow, hopelessness, and darkness were gone

It was then that I learnt from relationships
Therefore, gaining while learning from unhappy times and happy moments with others

Survivors

As a maple or willow would burst from the ground
I fell into a hole that was dark and dreary in the ground
There was not light even when darkness reeled in
I called for help, but no one came

As a maple or willow is subjected to sunlight, air, and water for its survival
These same forces can destroy these plants that grow to become trees

As a maple or willow would burst from the soil in the ground
I fell into a hole in the ground
One that I did not expect
One that I thought I would never leave
I called for help, but it never came
Until someone heard me cry then help would come

As a maple or willow stands by itself exposed to the elements of nature
It survives these same forces as destructive as they are on its own or by itself

Changing

I know I had to be a friend to myself
Rather than be my worst enemy
Why?
Using destroyed me!
While quitting healed me

Now I live and live without using
I am hopeful,
A success,
And stable

I am happy and healthy
I am positive and not negative
And nothing weighs me down as it picks me up

The Earth's Shadow Darkened Itself

In the darkness of night, it becomes darker
As the moon beams its light onto earth
The earth cast its shadow onto the moon
Causing an eclipse on the moon

Imagine, the earth's shadow darkening part of the moon
While the eclipse of the moon darkens part of the earth
As light becomes less
The earth is darkened by its own shadow

You Inspired Me to Succeed

You faltered while I fell
You gained but I struggled
Not knowing each other but carrying each other
Strangers who met briefly

Unknown to me you would become a success while I waited
But today I work as you have done
To become the one, I would like to be, a successful woman

Turning Pessimism into Optimism

*A negative self-concept turned me into a pessimist
Until I started believing this
Then I had to learn differently what optimism meant
To know what success could be*

*I knew I had been doing and learning
Without realizing that that was part of success in itself
Because I thought success meant having it all
Then I learnt it was living from day to day,
Learning every day,
And doing even more tomorrow*

*As I learnt I became an optimist
Adopting a positive self-concept
Bringing optimism into my life
As I learnt that success is doing
And doing even more leads to even greater success*

Two Souls Meant to Be

Two souls meet as one
In a place to themselves
Where heaven seemed to be?
The gateway to heaven opened for one soul to enter another soul
Love is not denied
Deeper and deeper these two souls meet
Reaching for the heavens!
Longing for the skies!
As these souls meet love is created for life to begin

Where Do I Belong?

A soul touched the earth's crust instead of heaven
He wondered what happened?
He looked to the sky!
Believing that was where he belonged
He said to himself its misery
Believing in one and not the other
Having been in hell
Now in between heaven and hell
A place called earth!

Continuing Without Misery

If life meant living for myself
I did not really know
It was not only about my-self
But meant relationships with others
Rather than with myself

Isolating myself would bring misery
That misery would not leave me
Because I carried it with me
It made me feel like I did not belong
Until I realized
I needed to reconnect with others

Reconnecting with others
Would mean rebuilding with others
Rebuilding these relationships
Would mean reestablishing with others

Difficulties would leave me as I learnt
Teaching me lessons
From life, love, and living

A Special Friend

Our paths met briefly
And you taught me
I learnt about misfortunes in life
But I learnt how to bounce-back
By healing myself and caring for myself
At times helping myself
We agreed!
But we disagreed?
About making improvements with myself
Even though I did?
Thanking you for being there when I needed you most

The Friends I Came to Know

Lost in doubt
But shocked with disbelief
I did not know what friendship meant
Until friends came with help

By teaching me more
I would learn more
And learning more
Would teach me more about myself

Therefore, their help I needed
Their help I received

Hell Was not for Me

Fire and brimstone were never thrown at me
Harsh words of harsh ways I experienced
Until the devil would not welcome me into his world
Because I was a stranger to him in his world
Why was I a stranger to him?
My ideas came from another world
While his ideas ruled his world?
With different ideas in a different world
I had to return to my world
Because there was no agreeing with the ideas of the
devil himself

Anticipation

Patience never ended
Because he knew of endearments, he experienced
He looked in a mirror
And saw someone else
He changed!
Learning about time, patience, and understanding
With time he proved himself
With patience he brought more into his life
And with understanding he would anticipate changes
for himself
By making commitments to be fulfilled

No Guilt No Shame

They did not ask why our love should be
Resentful or bitter souls attempted to destroy what they could not have
Resentful or bitter it was not theirs?
Our friendship bloomed while theirs died
Now questioning their motive to destroy what they never knew or had
I wondered why?
Still we did not know why with reasons so few
I asked again why were these bitter souls envious?
Our reasons to be together was simply ours not theirs

Not Using

If using was living
It did not help me
Therefore, I stopped
To improve my health
And to improve myself

Today I live without using,
Have a full life,
And have no regrets
One that I changed
One that will stay the same

Friendship Blues

A friend cried but I did not hear
Because I did not listen
Daunted by my reaction
He turned to me with a look of disappointment on his face
Why?
He gives almost always
I have given
But only when I chose too
This situation changed me
I listened the next time,
Heard what he had to say,
And understood he needed concern
While he needed it that way

What You Gave?

When, I needed?
You gave!
Giving meant I was receiving
All of yourself
But not from everyone

Time you had you shared
It did not matter where or when
You were there

Patience you had you showed
Listening meant I needed
Listening meant that you heard

Your understanding let me know you knew
At times when I did not know

Momma

I saw a thousand candles burn in your eyes at forty-two
At fifty-nine it was not there
I heard it in your voice
I did not see it in your eyes
As you laid?
You lied
You gave up
But we did not?
And I still did not know why?

The Depth of Friendship

*Friendships are deeper than other relationships
When there is understanding
It becomes a relationship
This I did not know
Until my friendships grew as they developed*

*Sometimes I wonder
What makes my friendships different?
Then again what are the elements of friendship?*

*Friends give love, support, understanding, attentiveness, and concern
The love we have as friends is not for ourselves but for each other
Support amongst each other includes listening as well as hearing
Understanding means knowing what the other person is experiencing
Attentiveness is sharing times together
And concern is all the time we care for each other*

Weathering the Storms

Days of thunder, rain, and lightening
Grumbling?
Pouring?
Striking?
I sensed, danger?

Not knowing when it would stop
Then it changed
The clouds cleared,
The rain disappeared,
And the rainbow appeared
Realizing I had survived danger
While weathering the storms

Altruistic

If altruism meant being generous
Then I did not know it
Because it meant being concerned
I am concerned and concerned about others
But I know I can be selfish too
The issues of others concern me
But generosity was something I knew
But I know I am still somewhat selfish too

Uncertainty

What didn't I know?
What didn't I believe?
What didn't I understand?
Undecided about knowing, believing, or understanding
I had to change!
But I knew something was lacking?
While something needed changing?
Ultimately learning!
Something did change

Someone That Was Hurt

Changes with my mind, body, and spirit
Would become cause for concern
My mind was scattered,
My body was weary,
And my spirit was unwell

My thoughts were scattered
That I misunderstood reality
Causing mental anguish

Exhausted till I was worn out
No longer could I endure the demands of it
Much less handle it

My spirit became unwell
By not realizing my feelings were leading me
To believe that I was not well

This would require intervention,
Evaluation,
Being admitted to,
And supervised for treatment to begin

Whom Do I Believe?

*Losing sight of myself may have appeared as mistakes
to others
But what others may have thought of me
May not have been the truth about me
If I had believed in what others thought of me
Then I would believe in what others did not know of me
Rather than believing in myself
If I believed in opinions
Then I would believe in what is untrue of me*

Phoolmatee Dubay

Ozone Depletion

Further north glaciers are shrinking
Occurring sooner than we thought
Our shores are not sea-beds
Yet!
Therefore, I question this!
Will I see this happen?
The effect of change can be good
But if we think it is bad
Then where can we move?

Being Given

He taught me the love of people,
The love of oneself,
And the love he needed in return
His means were love and compassion

He also taught me that tolerance was needed
Until it went away
His nature to nurture and care for others led me to him
This is when I found love to be him

Uncovered

I have walked this earth as you have
While you watched you waited
You uncovered what I wanted to know

Time did not stand still
It moved on as it ticked away
Waiting did not seem right?
Waiting did not seem wrong!

You walked this earth
But you still did not know I walked this earth too
It seemed like the times we were apart
We were heading in different directions
Not intended to meet but to come to an end

The Casino Life

Dollars and cents were spent on entertaining oneself
As a form of self-indulgence
Which drew me to the casino

The slots and table games did it for me
While money was spent to have more
But when it was gone it was over

Ten thousand to one said I did not know
But I have lost and won
Now knowing what winning or losing is

The Curse of Love

It is as if he cast a spell on me
Unknown to me
His love different when received
But the agony of waiting for his love is endearing
Or a test of time?
Until that time, we meet
I will know then
And I will know why
Your love is a curse in itself

The Loss of Time

It seems like I lose something when time passes
Unlike when I have time
I cannot wait for it to tick away
The loss of time?
Then again, I have time
One thing I realize is that time is precious
As much as we need it
The time we have is the time we have been given

Wake Up Call

It was a question in itself
Not for another but for myself
I will soon know what that will be
But it is not about someone else

It may be another role?
It may be another adventure?
Or it may become a resolution?
But when I wake up to this notion
I will then come to know my own decision

Envisioned

I lost vision for a moment in my head
It was not something about what I could not see
It was about losing sight of myself
I had envisioned many things for myself
But today it is all in the past
From today onwards I have new visions
As I move onwards

Despair Is Gone

With pitfalls came despair
My worth disappeared
Losing my income
Would amount to losses

Having no income meant I could not afford to live
With less I felt like an outcast
Where I longed for to return too

My independence would change to dependence
Making entitlements a way of life through needing
With less before but now I have more

My Quest

I searched my thoughts and wondered?
What have I stumbled upon?
What have I done?
What have I changed?

Not knowing myself seemed like mmmh...
I then touched my head,
Tumbled with ideas,
And still wondered?
What have I done?
What have I changed?

Missing You

Weeping did not bring you home
Emails I sent
You replied
That still did not return you
Yet I missed you?
Love I thought to be selfish
Only to realize it was you who did not understand your
commitments to me
I realized that you are significant to me
Was saying so a mistake?
Or did it meant missing you?

When Others Cared?

I did not notice I was hurting
Until others did
As lost as I was
I did not know for myself
Much less cared for myself

Others giving meant I needed
Their love and support would come as a surprise
I did not know I mattered
Until they gave
Letting me know
By letting it show

8:26 a.m.

Change brought esteem and confidence
Esteem brought respect
Confidence brought faith

Let Me Leave

As I walked away, I did not look back
But looked ahead
I left but it did not leave me
Because I walked away with you in me
Unknown to you I would keep your love safe
Hoping we will meet again
Somewhere?
Somehow?
Till then I still love holding on

Mirror

I investigated a mirror and saw myself as a
woman of change
With long black hair, brown eyes, and brown skin
But I also realized changes
My hair had turned gray to the front of my head,
I looked older than I thought,
And I had gained too much weight around my mid-section
With this realization I became displeased with myself
Deciding to improve my appearance
I would lose ten pounds
But I would not dye my hair
Because I am yet to make that decision

Wanting Something but Needing Something Else

I looked at you
Because I heard it in your voice
And saw it in your eyes
These signs told me that you were hurt
But if I had not seen or heard it
I would not have known it
Compassion I gave
But love is what you needed
Comforting you at that moment held you together
But later I understood that love was the answer
Unknown to me and still unaware that you needed more
I could not have guessed until you reached for me and
asked for more

Flower Petals

Women are like flowers
But I wonder what type am I?
I simply know women are like flowers
But which one is each one?
For there are many species of flowers
But I wonder which one am I?
Because I am yet to know
I wonder if compared to a flower how would you describe me?
Bright or colorful?
Scented or beautiful?

What Inspires Me?

Have a real friend listen to your needs
And you will know what true friendship means
Listen to your favorite music
And you will tune in to thoughts you love
Get up early one morning and watch the sun rise
And you will see the beginning of a new day
Then what inspires me is not what is in me
But what is outside of myself

Enrichment

A meaningful life meant living a fuller life
But somehow, I felt I needed to enrich myself
Enrichment came from people, places, and events

Enrichment would come from the knowledge of others
Learning brought understanding
Understanding brought meaning
And meaning would bring knowledge

Places visited had stories of their own
With different landmarks and history
For those who had occupied
And for those who still occupy these towns

Events were part of cultures
Those were opportunities for me to learn about languages, cuisines, clothing, and customs
Languages taught me how we speak
Cuisines are what we eat
Clothing is what we wear
And customs are our beliefs

Who Are These Men?

Men hurt by reasons that were real to them
And hurt by others for not understanding whom they were
As a group of men with passion for others
And a love of music
They changed?
Exploring, learning, gaining, and earning
Acquiring fame, fans, and fortunes
With friends and family at their side
Making themselves men of worth today
As they were yesterday

He's Unknown to You but Known to Me

A gentle soul with gentle ways
A harsh reality made him a winner
A lady's man to women
A giver not a taker
By giving to another he would expect in return
A friend to none but to everyone
This makes him a man to be who he is
And not what he is known for

What We Have?

Yesterday I felt like I did not have much
But tomorrow I will see myself as having more
But today I will earn for tomorrow all that I need
Having less does not mean that I do not have
Setbacks were apparent while doing and achieving
Pushed back but I pressed on

Sometimes Its' Not for Always

Pushed into the midst of a moment
I was taken by surprise
He said what love might be
Still not believing in what he said
He did not understand my reaction because of a blank face

He then turned to me and said this is for you
A symbol of love
Still not believing in what he said
It was then that I understood the reaction he might
have expected
In reply he said he could not wait for me to decide
Now understanding what he meant
I turned to him and said I never knew

Reflections of Time

A year has past
With much to speak of and reflect about
But today it becomes memories of yesteryear
This includes having held on to my friends
And not losing any loved ones this past year

Instead I gained
How?
I regained my health,
Wrote a book of poems,
And continued to make things happen
In the process of doing so I recognized myself
As a woman who has reflected

Needing Friends and Friends Needing Me

Selfish at times
Only understanding myself
I have gotten from others
But I have not given as much
You may think of it as a selfish act
Or a selfish motive
A crime you may think I have committed
Until this hour
Then I would know that friends need love at this hour

Emotions Stirred

Once a lady now a woman
I became a woman before I knew it
One said I had become an old woman
But I see myself as being a woman of experience
His loss may have been my gain?
I guess?
I ventured!
Therefore, I gained

Embedded Within

As a child I did not understand life
As a teen I still did not know life
As an adult then it seemed like I began to understand the secrets of life
Today, in middle-adulthood I have come to know, understand, and learn as I've changed

As a child life seemed like an adventure
To explore, learn, and know
I remember what I remember
Going to elementary school, home, and my neighborhood

As a teen I had to change in secondary school because I was ridiculed for being heavy
Too fat?
I changed!
Diet, exercise, and running changed the fat girl into a lovely young lady

As an adult I had to learn to earn everything that I wanted and needed
This included being responsible for family obligations as well as my own obligations
Today I live apart from family being the one responsible for everything, if anything in my life

Where is Home?

Is it where I live today?
Was it where I lived a decade ago?
Or was it where I lived twenty years ago?

Today I share an apartment with roommates
Not out of shame but out of necessity
I like it but sometimes I love it
With my space, time, and energy I do reflect about
years gone by

A decade ago, I shared an apartment with relatives
Home for a while in someone else's home
Home with love for a moment
Then it turned out to be my time to depart from their home

Twenty years ago, I lived with my siblings and parents
A home of love, comfort, compassion, and tolerance
Only to be pushed away to be here today

Friends for A Moment

Once lost!
I saw a stranger that needed a friend
By noticing his hurt
A man too hurt to not know
I looked at him to melt his fears
Which he did not expect?
Which he did not know?
Then our eyes met
Reassuring him
While giving him

Will I Thrive?

I am surviving while others are flourishing
I long to prosper but I am only a survivor
I wonder why is this so?
Am I paying attention to what I do?
Or am I wasting my time?
As others succeed, advance, and prosper I struggle
What does this mean?
Am I a failure?
I watch others succeed
Do I wait for it to happen?
What is that they do that I do not do?
Will I learn but when?
Will I ever conquer my failure as success?

On My Way to Connecticut

Traveling north
Looking east
The east coast shorelines were not what I thought it to be
But an unfolding body of water
With rivers flowing to the sea

Then looking south
With the sun setting west
I wondered with amazement!

Obligations

These are my commitments
Writing the love of words
To convey thoughts and ideas,
To inspire,
To remember,
And to heal
Not just for one but for many as well

Remember or Forget?

As I recall I remember
When I do not remember I forget
I wonder if it is what I chose by selecting that makes the difference
Why is it that I remember some things while I forget others?
Good times I remember
Bad times I forget

The good times were not painful moments
These were moments I still cherish today
For instance, I enjoyed my youth with friends with a carefree attitude

Bad times meant difficult times with painful moments
I dealt with each painful moment by burying it
And holding onto it

When I think of good times?
I am happy
When I think of bad times?
I feel miserable
The question about how I think, or feel is dependent on what I recall

Anchored

Did living make me a casualty of life?
Or becoming a victim of circumstances meant that I
was living?
Or was I misunderstood?

As a casualty of life
Life did not seem fair to me
I felt like I had failed to live up to my own expectations

As a victim of circumstances
I made choices that backfired
Causing me to be burnt
Then becoming scarred

If I was misunderstood?
I did not know it or realize it
But today I still stand tall
As I learnt that I had to grow, know, and understand myself

The Unknown of Depth

As I was submerged
I was sinking
Caught in the tides of danger
I thought it to be the end
Then something happened?
I started to rise to the surface
Still thinking it was the end
Until I reached the surface with the core untouched
I emerged!
Then realizing I had survived the dangers of depth

I Found My Way Home

I did not know home began with myself
Retracing my steps meant I did not know
Because I did not believe
Home seemed to be with family
But friends and others I needed
While I felt distant from home
I felt close to them

Time Is Ageless

As ever present is time
Across decades throughout centuries before
Man has documented time by measuring it
An asset to man time has become

As ageless time is
People are not
But as time has passed it has aged

Why Hurt?

Hurt is something invisible to the eye
But we can feel it
When it hurts?
We hurt!
It is difficult to understand at times
Especially when it hurts to the point of tears

I know when I hurt, I cry silently to myself while I
shed tears
There are various reasons why we hurt
It may include the loss of a loved one
Or it may be the end of a relationship
Or it may even be extending oneself to another in their
time of need

It can also be endearing at times
But hurt can be eased
Because it is only temporary as I have experienced
It was only then that I realized
It is just that way

The Woman

She rises at six every morning
Brews herself a cup of coffee to awaken her-self
She sips it for fifteen minutes without thinking about much

To make the coffee she adds two teaspoons of instant coffee,
Two teaspoons of sugar,
Two ounces of milk,
And six ounces of hot water
Then it turns out to be eight ounces of coffee
She makes for herself every morning

Bouncing Back

I will face the world,
Speak from the heart,
And say I am back
I will say I have risen above many situations
You may ask why I hope
I had to deal with deception that may have
stemmed from lies
This may have been a way of life for others but not for me
I took a different course in life that took me in a
different direction
Gaining a perspective of life
I did not know was mine
Challenged again!
Will I face deception?
Or will I misunderstand their intentions?

When Momma Cried

I remember seeing her tears
And wondering why
Unknown to me
She was hurt
When I looked at her again

I had seen her cry many times
But still did not understand
Why?
Her hurt baffled me throughout the years
Hoping I would not hurt that much
But later experiencing the same hurt
While silently crying to myself

My Worth as A Woman

I have not been a wife or a mother
But I have been a sister to my siblings,
A daughter to my parents,
A friend to my friends,
And a lover to my lover
Those were and still are significant roles I play

I have been a caregiver and a helper
As a caregiver I have cared for others
As a helper I have helped others
Now at 46, I am still a sister, a daughter, a friend, and not a lover
But I still care for others when I give and when I help

Today my views have changed
The lives of others matter more so today
Than yesterday
At once I placed success before the needs of people
But now I realize that concern must be first
Especially for those whose needs are to be met

Ten Things I Never Knew

I had to fly
Had to head north
Departed
Arrived
Drove to a house they called home
But it was not mine
Then I died
I was not buried
But then I had to come alive

Self- Examination

What is life?
Is it living?
Is it running a twenty-six-mile marathon?
Is it marrying to have a husband?
Or is it living for oneself?
I have lived but not for everyone
But I have lived for my friends
And I have lived for my family
Had I not done this then I would not have been me

Six Miracles

Four plus two equals six
As numbers they add up to all my siblings and myself
Each one is unique to me
As I am unique to them
My siblings taught me about love, kindness, and concern
As each one has extended himself or herself as true
siblings would

A Dark Place in My Head

As dark as an abyss in the mind where no light shines
Even in the presence of light
What made it this way?
I asked!
If it is not known for light to be present in darkness
Then in light it becomes even darker

Troubled

The chime moves with the sound of the wind
Water runs and flows into the sea
As tears flow down my cheeks
At the sound of my cries
For I have lost someone that I thought loved me
Why me?
I did not know
Because I could not see
I could only wonder
How could this be?

I Could not See

Until you came, saw, and said to me
How unsure can you be?
Till the day I saw
I wondered if it hurt more
Until now I did not know, I did not hear, or I did not see
Until I cried
Tears you did not hear
And could not see
Because you did not know

The Rising Sun

As I rise
So does the sun
I crawl out of bed
But you hide behind clouds
You rise, but I do not know why
Your light comes through my window
Yet it could be brighter
Come?
And come as you should
To show me your power that lights my soul

Until This Hour

Needing something but not knowing at the same time
Seemed far away
Then I began to wonder when would it happen for me?
As I wait or as I see it happen?
Becoming impatient but still not knowing
Then I started undermining the importance of needing
Yet still not knowing

Seasonal Changes

I shiver during winter, but I do not during summer
Whereas the leaves return in spring but leaves us in autumn
As seasons change, we adapt

In winter I wear a coat, hat, gloves, and shoes to fit
the weather
In summer I wear shorts and t-shirts or dresses
with sandals
In spring I wear slacks or long dresses with a spring
jacket and flats
In fall I wear a coat, a pair of jeans, sweater, and
boots of choice
Wearing these attire shows that I have learnt about
seasonal changes
As to what I should or should not wear

But sometimes I wish summer and spring would never end
And fall and winter would never return
But then again, we would not have a white Christmas
Much less a colorful fall

Limitations

*Once limited
Then I discovered more potential than I knew
I became enthusiastic again*

*At once limitations made me feel like I did not know much
As I woke up to this notion
I changed my ideas about myself
Realizing I could do more for myself
As well as for others
Then I would come to know my own potential*

Can I Set Free of My Past?

My past is still a part of me
Which are moments I could not change
I see it as my history
It molded me because I have grown from it
As I have evolved from it
Each experience would become the influence I needed
To change my opinion of myself
Teaching me of who I am not
But teaching me of who I am

Now You are Gone

I did not know it hurt to bring us up
I did not know the pain you endured
Much less understanding your roles as our parents
We have grown from growing up
Some are here
Some are gone
Today I have come to know and understand what both of
you have done
You made us all
Because we are here as well as alive
We came into this world because of you
We did not know what it meant to have both of you
Until now

Caged or Confined?

I dreamt of birds
In a large cage
That appeared red, green, yellow, blue, and pink?
Seemingly disturbed by something
That I thought they needed to escape

A moment later I felt something dropped on me in my dreams
As I opened my eyes in this dream
I saw one of the birds on me
One that was hurt
One that would die

It was unclear what this meant
But I felt there were too many birds in that cage
Had I not awakened from the dream
I would have opened the cage and set them free

When Eyes Smile?

If misery held me up
It must have held me together
Today it brought relief
And that became a sign that something had changed
Sometimes I think I see it in my eyes
But only for a moment
I hope that that moment could bring me to myself
While my misery is gone

Solitude

If alienating myself meant eliminating doubts
Then it became a situation that made me sorry
It turned out to be a time of isolation
That became time that I felt I had wasted
And time that I felt I had lost
But years later I stopped wasting my time
By not doubting myself
Therefore, changing, recovering, and returning to living
By having more to see and more to do

Many Best Friends

I have few friends that are best friends
I would not change for any reason
Their friendships I value
But during difficult times they just help
While in happier times they just give
Does helping and giving of themselves demonstrates their care and concern for me?
While I hope I do as much for each one as they have done for me

I Deal with Life

I could not see life for what it was
Therefore, how could I accept it for what it is?
And not for what it is not
When I did not know I had doubts
But now I know I have answers
This does not mean that doubts are gone
Because I still need answers
Even while looking at life differently

Authors of Influence

I have read what they have written
To understand their work
Amazed with their writing skills
All winners of achievements
Men to admire for their integrity
Men who have become well established
Men who faced adversities
But benefited from these adversities
While overcoming and achieving

Proving Oneself

If succeeding meant failing
Then you may think I have never known true success
This may be true?
Or this may be false?
But progress has been made in ways that count

Prisoner of Pain

My body felt like prison walls that held my pain
It seemed like the pain had been held in forever
Confined for reasons beyond my comprehension
I have longed to escape these prison walls many times
I asked myself why is this so?
Did these walls make me a prisoner of crimes I have committed?
Were these crimes of the heart?
Or crimes of the soul?
Or is it solace I seek to let go?
Or not to be alone?

Motivation

When I felt discouraged it never mattered
While discouraged I did nothing
Why did I feel this way?
I did not know!
Then how was I encouraged to be motivated?

I found out I had to let someone know
I turned to professionals
Then I turned to family members
But still did not know

Then I turned to a stranger who had been there
But was not discouraged
His notions would become ideas I would follow
Not discouraged but encouraged

Then I met another whose views would change me
He would mentor me
Causing me to explore
Then realizing what both had done
Brought awareness and undying gratitude
That still motivates me today

The Flame

As a candle burns it gives light in darkness
While in my darkness there was no light
As the flame flickered it went out
Then I would feel pain while it hurt
While I hurt, I did not trust to let anyone know
At that point I would need a shoulder while I needed a heart
On that shoulder I would lean on while I cried
With that heart I would need care
Without a shoulder or a heart
I would bleed
Now I have a shoulder
And a heart that heals

Giving Is A Way of Life

*I did not know extending oneself happens everywhere in
my presence
This was not an observation
But something others do without thinking
Some may think it is an option
But for others it is a way of life*

*I did not believe I was given much
Because I felt I had done enough
I realized giving entailed helping others while earning
something of value
Things of value earned could be money, experience, or
making a difference*

*Money could be the incentive to work but it means
more than that
Because in some professions helping others is a way of life
This may include being a nurse or a doctor*

*Giving is one-way of gaining
Without expecting
Volunteering is giving of your time to assist others*

*Making a difference is helping others to survive
Natural disasters
While lending a hand to rebuild*

Welcome Home!

I am a veteran of a war that never ended
I lost a limb and four fingers
Because of explosives nearby

While the war is ongoing
I faced a different battle that will stay with me
and never end
My wounds will heal but the scars will remain

There was no parade when I arrived home
But my friends and family members
Realizing in every battle we lose something of ourselves

The Reality That I Face Today or The Next Day

I get up every morning just like everyone else,
I face the world,
And I prepare myself for the day's activities
But before I do this
I transform myself into a woman that prepares to do
Then the day begins
Activities may differ each day
Because some days I work
While on other days I am at home

What I've Been Through as Opposed to Overcoming It

Addictions caused symptoms
Symptoms became insanity
Insanity would become a diagnosis
Needing treatment for the rest of my life

This may sound simple
But the truth of the matter is that I experienced hell
While not knowing or understanding my illness
I had to learn
And learn about the dangers and harm from using
But today I do not use
As I progress each day

I Learnt Through Sharing

Unknown to me someone wasn't listening
The unsaid had to be said
But it was still unknown to others

Then I met someone whom I could confide in
I had problems
He had solutions

Another came along
While I had questions
He had answers

It was then that I learnt
If I had not shared
I would not have known more than my own misery

Our Time

As adults we indulged in exploring possibilities
Those possibilities may include helping others
But then something happened?
We changed!
I came out of my insanity,
Another discovered healing,
And the other found love in himself

The answers were not found or discovered separately
It was a question of trusting each other but not hurting each other
We all had had enough of pain and misery
While deciding to deal with the hurt
But not without disclosing while in pain

Fortunately, we knew enough to withstand while we understood
Because the time had arrived to be dealt with
Then this became our time to overcome

Phoolmatee Dubay

A Friend to Admire

His name is not to be mentioned because he said so
He has given as well as gotten
He does not demand the worst
He simply asks for the best
He has ideas unknown to me but known to him
His ideas are of his experiences from adversities
Which he overcame?
Through learning and learning even more

A Changed Man!

Once angry
Once sad
He did not know who to turn too
And this left him longing for arms of comfort
Because an embrace he wanted while he needed

Needing was one thing
But embracing him would be another
This would be the beginning of understanding
Then accepting meant that he knew
Therefore, he changed

Prey and Predator

A prey is a victim
While the predator is one that preys on its victim
At once I thought of myself as being a victim
Somewhat like a prey
The predator on the other hand were humans
Veracious to know
But sought to exploit me for not knowing my way
Misunderstood again by others
I had to walk away to begin again
Becoming a victim of circumstances
With lessons that I learnt

Running Away

Could not face it
Therefore, I ran from it
Troubled or not?
I could not handle much less deal with
Today that has changed
Because I know now
I cope with life
I deal with life
The difference today is knowing rather than not knowing
Allowing me to have learnt the difference

Mentoring Me

You motivated me
When I did not know or understand
You helped me
But I had to help me too

Your guidance I needed
While it lasted
A brief time
With much explored
With much gained

The Journey

I will ride the train
The train will stop several times
I will get there later
While I will travel through Farmingdale, Minneola, and Nassau County
I will look through the window as if it were a movie
Just reeling as the train heads for my destination
That destination will be Montauk and I will be there soon
The trip is now nearing its end
And I will see him after all
For the first time in my life

Finding Answers Within Myself

Reflecting taught me
That answers are within me
To bring changes
But today I felt guilt
Until I realized I needed to be myself
Not someone I am supposed to be

Comforting Words

A reminder of good things
And the benefits of overcoming
Brought a new outlook
This shed light into my life
As I remember in my youth
The presence of friends
Spending time with each other
Out or at home

Monday Was Not Friday

A new week began today
But yesterday I did not feel that way
Then what did I do?
I turned to a friend
As I know listens
But not when I speak words through facial expressions
She would look at me
And then say
You know you give
Just ask when you need

Locked in My Room

I looked at the clock that tells no time
Then my eyes shifted its focus from left to right
Looking at what surrounded me
It was then that I saw
A bookcase with books of interest on the shelves
The bed in my room had no sheets on it
The draws of the dresser were filled with things like sheets and towels
While on the dresser had perfume, skin lotions, lipsticks, and various colors of nail polish
Inside my wardrobe had clothing on hangers
It was then that I realized I owned these things

Cruelty to Oneself

Today I wonder why I used and abused
Was I a fool?
Or was I misinformed?

I recall someone telling me
Do not drink or do not smoke
If abusing myself was not right
I did not know

I still question
How misinformed could I have been?
The consequences of using
Brought misconceptions of reality,
Emotional setbacks,
And physical ailments

Impatience

Others say wait
I say no!
Why?
I may have time
But I have ideas
These ideas can be developed sooner than others know
But I get feedback that spells wait
But waiting seems so far away?
While I feel as if I have produced more than I knew
or realized
But still I know I must wait
Yet I am impatient?
This makes me realize that dreams take time
But I know I can make it happen

A Unique Experience Is Life

Setbacks were ailments that hurt
Looking back, I see it as a means that supplemented experiences
It hurt but I overcame to carry on
The pain I forget
But the memories I remember
I know I cannot change these moments as memories
But I can say I have lived

A True Friend

He gives without asking
But he wants in return
I give, and he gets
We agree at times
While we disagree at times
This is just a little of what friendship is
But it means more
It means lending an ear when needed
It means extending care, concern, and compassion as well
With all this in a friend you would think we knew
each-other?
Well?
We do!

Finding True Love

My search led me
From the Red Sea to the Black Sea
That search ended
When it became you

I thought I had known love
But now I have found love
A love that says you
A love that says me
And love that says we

Now that it is us
It is here
I thought I could only wish for

Once a vision
Now a dream
Then a reality
That has become real

Did Not Know Love

Went from one to another
Choosing through listening
Understanding through needing
It would change
Until now

Wanting for myself
Never knowing if it would stay
Never knowing if it would last
I would give love
As I received love

Who Brought Love

Tall, dark, and unknown
Not too shy
Not too bold
But just, right

Turning heads
While turning mines
Captured by his ways
Captured by his words

Who would have thought it would be me?
Who could have thought it would be you?
A man to many
But boy to me

I did not think I could get you
But now I have you

Living

At once I thought living meant dying
Then I thought I could live
Then I found myself surviving
And then succeeding

Being alive meant coming alive
This meant I was living and breathing
Not because of me
But because of others

Now that I know what living means
I will stay and not leave
Until I decide to depart
Not before leaving my trademark

Phoolmatee Dubay

The Professor of Love

When I hurt
You love!
When I want love
You give love
Then I am not without love
But if something changes
You still love

Andrew

A friend, a healer, a father, and a husband
As a friend he gives and gives without asking
As a healer he listens and listens well
As a father he nurtures and nurtures well
As a husband he loves and loves well

Who Stole My Heart?

It is as if I committed a crime
Asking for his
But instead he stole mines

Not knowing if he is coming or going
He steals it every time
In my presence
Or even when he is away

His victim I became
When he asked me to carry his name?
My response was
I did not think that you would

Developments

I found myself
I found a mate
I have friends
I have family
I have success
I have money
I have love

What more could I want for myself?
What else could I ask for?
I just want to be around for years
To enjoy all that I have and earn more
But help others as well

My Resurrection

Small ideas but with big passion
Determined to change
Determined to succeed
A voice yet to be heard
But with ideas of my own
I will be known

Once my aim
But now my game
I will play it
Then I will know it
Do not play it
Then I will not know it

Once buried alive
Now I have come alive

Doing Right by Others

*Once others thought I did wrong
But I did not think so
I needed to live to know
Not to be told I should not know
Loving one seemed wrong at once
It hurt
But it taught me that he hurt too*

*Now I know we should live and let others live
Without doing so
What's life for then?
I would think to live and know
But also, to live and learn*

Do not Judge Me

If what is written and said about me is true
Then what is wrong with me?
Leave me
Not judge me
For I am only myself
I would rather be I and be myself

Being Gracious Too

I am not a queen
But a woman of love
Because of injury I once hurt
But that did not stop me
Instead it helped me

I learnt to love me
Then I learnt to love others
Because sometimes I think I see others hurt
Then I run to their side
Then I run to their aide
I help if they need
And I help if they ask

Healing Helps

My wounds hurt
I hurt from hurting
I need your compassion
I need your love
I need you

But then I find that you need
Do you hurt as well?
Or is it that we hurt as well?
Then what do we do?
What can we do?

We need not say it
Because we feel it
And we see it

Coming Out of The Dark

I had to hurt again
To know again
But it is not only me that feels
Everyone does
Then how could I be so blind?

Now that I know
It can happen again
I will hurt again
But I will know again

I would not die if it happens
There are reasons for this
Others are human
And human again

What's Owed?

I have earned but have I given?
I have gotten but have I given?
Yet I want and want more
Is this selfish?
Or is it just this way?

What I earn is not enough
But I share
What I have gotten is adequate
But I am yet to give
I do not control it
Because I do not have it
But I will
Soon?

I Will for You

I did not know where to start
Much less where to begin
That I would find myself second-guessing
Trying to find out
Trying to know
Now that I know
There is no guessing

Broken Wings

I attempt to fly
But with torn feathers
I cannot
Repair my wings
That takes me to the sky
For which I cannot do
Heal my wings
To soar again
As high as I can

www.ingramcontent.com/pod-product-compliance
Lightning Source LLC
LaVergne TN
LVHW091557060526
838200LV00036B/873